It's My
STATE!

MASSACHUSETTS
The Bay State

Elizabeth Schmermund,
Ruth Bjorklund, and
Stephanie Fitzgerald

Cavendish
Square
New York

Published in 2019 by Cavendish Square Publishing, LLC
243 5th Avenue, Suite 136, New York, NY 10016

Fourth Edition

Website: cavendishsq.com

This publication represents the opinions and views of the author based on his or her personal experience, knowledge, and research. The information in this book serves as a general guide only. The author and publisher have used their best efforts in preparing this book and disclaim liability rising directly or indirectly from the use and application of this book.
All websites were available and accurate when this book was sent to press.

Library of Congress Cataloging-in-Publication Data
Names: Schmermund, Elizabeth, author. | Bjorklund, Ruth, author. | Fitzgerald, Stephanie, author.
Title: Massachusetts / Elizabeth Schmermund, Ruth Bjorklund, and Stephanie Fitzgerald.
Description: New York : Cavendish Square, 2019. | Series: It's my state! (fourth edition) |
Includes bibliographical references and index. | Audience: Grades 3-5.
Identifiers: LCCN 2017051572 (print) | LCCN 2017052396 (ebook) | ISBN 9781502626301 (library bound) |
ISBN 9781502626165 (ebook) | ISBN 9781502644435 (pbk.)
Subjects: LCSH: Massachusetts--Juvenile literature.
Classification: LCC F64.3 (ebook) | LCC F64.3 .S36 2019 (print) | DDC 974.4--dc23
LC record available at https://lccn.loc.gov/2017051572

Editorial Director: David McNamara
Editor: Caitlyn Miller
Copy Editor: Nathan Heidelberger
Associate Art Director: Alan Sliwinski
Designer: Jessica Nevins
Production Coordinator: Karol Szymczuk
Photo Research: J8 Media

Printed in the United States of America

It's My STATE!

Table of Contents

MASSACHUSETTS

The Bay State

State Flag

The state flag of Massachusetts displays the state seal on a white background. Unlike the seal, though, the phrase "Sigillum Reipublicae Massachusettensis" is not present on the flag.

Statehood

February 6, 1788

Population

6,859,819
(2017 census estimate)

Capital

Boston

State Song

"All Hail to Massachusetts" by Arthur J. Marsh is the official song of the state. Beginning with the lyrics "All hail to Massachusetts, the land of the free and the brave!" the tune became the official state song in 1966. In 1981, Arlo Guthrie's "Massachusetts" was named as the state's official folk song.

HISTORICAL EVENTS TIMELINE

1620
Plymouth Colony is established by the Pilgrims.

1629
The Massachusetts Bay Colony is established by the English.

1773
The Boston Tea Party takes place. It involves colonists dumping tea into Boston Harbor to protest taxes they consider unfair.

State Seal

The state seal of Massachusetts shows a Native American man holding a bow and arrow on a blue background with a white star to represent the state. The arrow is pointed down to represent peace and not war. A blue ribbon around the seal bears the Latin words "Ense petit placidam sub libertate quietem." This phrase means, "By the sword we seek peace, but peace only under liberty." The words "Sigillum Reipublicae Massachusettensis" circle the seal. The English translation is "Seal of the Republic of Massachusetts."

State Tree

America Elm

The American elm was named the official state tree in 1941. The tree was chosen to **commemorate** the moment General George Washington took command of American troops. He did so under an American elm in Cambridge Common in 1775.

One famous American elm from Massachusetts, the Liberty Tree, is shown here.

1775

The Battles of Lexington and Concord start the Revolutionary War.

1788

Massachusetts becomes the sixth state.

1820

Massachusetts and Maine are separated into two states.

State Flower

Mayflower

The mayflower is the state flower of Massachusetts. The flower shares its name with the ship that first brought European settlers, known as Pilgrims, to Plymouth Rock in 1620. It bears light pink or white flowers.

State Cookie

Chocolate Chip Cookie

State Dog

Boston Terrier

2003

The *Boston Globe*'s famous Spotlight investigative team wins the newspaper its sixteenth Pulitzer Prize.

2004

Same-sex marriage rights are approved in the state; the Boston Red Sox win their first World Series since 1918, breaking the "Curse of the Bambino."

2006

Governor Mitt Romney passes sweeping health-care reform. These policies are later used as a template for the Affordable Care Act.

State Marine Mammal

Right Whale

State Bird

Black-Capped Chickadee

CURRENT EVENTS TIMELINE

2007
Deval Patrick becomes the first African American governor of Massachusetts.

2013
The Boston Marathon bombing on April 15 kills 3 people and injures 264.

2017
The New England Patriots win Super Bowl LI. The victory is the team's fifth Super Bowl win.

From the Bridge of Flowers in Shelburne Falls, visitors can see the Berkshire Hills and the Deerfield River. Massachusetts has beautiful scenery in every region of the state.

1 Geography

The geography of Massachusetts has always been important to the culture and history of the state. Its coastline drew some of the earliest European settlers. In modern day, the fall colors in Massachusetts draw visitors from around the world.

The name "Massachusetts" comes from the Massachuset tribe, who took their name from an expression meaning "by the great hill." Indeed, rolling green hills cover much of the state—from the Eastern Seaboard to the Berkshire Hills in the west.

Massachusetts is part of New England, a region in the northeastern part of the country that also includes Connecticut, Rhode Island, Vermont, New Hampshire, and Maine. Massachusetts contains fourteen counties. Boston, the state's capital and largest city, is part of Suffolk County in the eastern part of the state.

FAST FACT

Lowell, Massachusetts, was America's first planned industrial city. It was incorporated in 1826 as a mill town. Lowell later became a hub of the Industrial Revolution due to its textile factories.

Massachusetts borders New Hampshire, Vermont, Connecticut, Rhode Island, and New York.

At just 7,800 square miles (20,202 square kilometers), Massachusetts is a small state. However, it has a wide variety of landforms. In fact, it has more than any other New England state. Massachusetts has many types of beaches. Some are sandy and flat. Others are rocky and steep. Rivers flow throughout the state, including New England's largest, the Connecticut River. There are mountain ranges, rolling farmlands, sand dunes, swamps, lakes, and forests.

The Berkshires

The peak of Mount Greylock features the War Memorial Tower.

The scenic Berkshire Hills in western Massachusetts are a great place to enjoy the brilliant colors of fall. Hardwood trees such as oak, beech, maple, and white birch cover the hills. When the weather cools, the leaves turn many shades of yellow, red, and gold.

When it was first formed, the Berkshire mountain range featured sharp and jagged peaks. After millions of years, however, wind, ice, and water wore away the peaks. Eventually, they were worn down to only the hardest

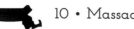

rock, creating the rounded hills that exist today. Because the ground is rugged and the soil is poor, few people have farmed this region. Beavers, bobcats, wild turkeys, snowshoe hares, porcupines, black bears, and mink live in the Berkshires. Nearby are two large river valleys, the Hoosic and the Housatonic. These valleys feature wonderful white-water rapids, waterfalls, and sheer walls of marble, quartz, and granite. Mount Greylock, the state's highest peak, rises here. The mountain reaches 3,491 feet (1,064 meters) at its **summit**.

The Housatonic River is 148 miles (238 kilometers) long.

The Connecticut River Region

The Connecticut River runs north to south for 68 miles (109 kilometers) through the center of Massachusetts. The river flows by fertile farms, wetlands, dinosaur-footprint fossils, and a three-hundred-million-year-old lava flow. Not far from the Connecticut River is a valuable natural resource called Quabbin Reservoir. In the 1930s, Boston and other big cities wanted to dam a river because they needed more fresh water. Officials asked the citizens of four nearby towns to relocate. They agreed. Their houses and businesses were moved by truck. Workers built a dam, which helped flood the abandoned towns. Today, migrating birds along with deer, coyotes, and eagles flock to Quabbin Reservoir. This wildlife refuge is full of color in spring.

The Connecticut River flows through the center of Massachusetts.

The Quabbin Reservoir

The Massachusetts Bay Colony

In 1625, Charles I became king of England. He believed in ruling the country as he saw fit. He created many enemies in the Church of England when he began to pass laws restricting certain religious groups, including the Puritans. The Puritans were Protestants who wanted to "purify" or reform the Church of England. As the Puritans became more and more restricted under Charles I's rule in England, they decided they must leave. John White, a Puritan minister, began to seek funding to start a colony. Then, on March 19, 1628, a **land grant** was issued to start a territory between the Charles and Merrimack Rivers in modern-day Massachusetts.

King Charles I allowed the New England Company to create a colony at Massachusetts Bay.

That same year, the New England Company for a **Plantation** in Massachusetts Bay sent about one hundred settlers to the region. The colony's first governor made the journey with the group. The New England Company still needed approval from the king so that there would be no competing claims on their land. In 1629, they got their wish. King Charles I granted a new **charter**. It formally established the new colony at Massachusetts Bay.

Experts think that Charles did not know that Puritans had settled the colony to escape his rule. Part of the charter says:

The [colony] established at Plymouth, in the County of Devon, for the planting, ruling, ordering, and governing of New England in America, have by their Deed, indented under their Common Seal, bearing Date the nineteenth Day of March last past, … [been] given … all that part of New England in America aforesaid, which lies and extends between a great River there commonly called … Merrimack, and a certain other river there, called Charles River, being in the bottom of a certain Bay there, commonly called Massachusetts, … and also all … those lands and [property that can be inherited] whatsoever, lying within the space of three English miles on the south part of the said Charles River … and also, all those lands and [property that can be inherited] whatsoever, which lie, and be within the space of three English miles to the Northward of the said River called … Merrimack."

The land described in the charter that made up the Massachusetts Bay Colony was supposed to be under the rule of Charles I. However, the Puritans who continued to come to the colony used Charles I's charter as the beginning of their own constitution. They established self-rule. The Massachusetts Bay Colony—which included the cities of Boston and Salem—was combined with the territories of the Plymouth Colony, Maine, Nantucket, and Martha's Vineyard in 1691.

Boston Harbor

That's also when thousands of dragonflies and butterflies gather.

Heading East

Although eastern Massachusetts is the most populated area of the state, it has lots of natural places to explore. Along the North Shore, birders come from all over the world to watch for the thousands of shorebirds that live in the marshes, sand dunes, and wetlands. The fishing communities of Gloucester and Rockport are located on Cape Ann, which juts into the sea. From Cape Ann to north of Boston, the coastline is rocky, with many small islands. Boston and its far-reaching suburbs are built along the shores of Boston Harbor. Two major rivers, the Mystic and the Charles, flow into the harbor. During the last ice age, which ended about 11,500 years ago, glaciers covered the coastline from what is now Boston to Cape Cod, carving out ponds, rock ledges, and river valleys. When Earth's climate warmed,

Visitors from all over go to Pilgrim Memorial State Park to see Plymouth Rock.

Visiting Walden Pond

In the 1840s, writer Henry David Thoreau spent two years at Walden Pond in Concord, Massachusetts. He lived in a small, one-room house that he built with his own hands. The experience inspired him to write *Walden*—an American classic. In the book, Thoreau details his simple life in the natural landscape.

Today, it is possible to visit Walden Pond and see where Thoreau lived. The grounds are now a state reservation that cover 462 acres (187 hectares). Visitors can fish in the lake or enjoy the natural surroundings on a hike. A 1.7 mile (2.7 km) trail skirts the edge of the lake. Many other paths wind through the nearby woods.

Visitors can also learn more about Thoreau in the visitor center. There is even a replica of Thoreau's cabin, so visitors can experience just how modestly Thoreau lived.

Walden Pond offers walking trails, boating, and a visitor center.

To explain why he lived at Walden Pond, Thoreau wrote, "I went to the woods because I wished to live deliberately, to front only the essential facts of life, and see if I could not learn what it had to teach, and not, when I came to die, discover that I had not lived." On the grounds of Walden Pond State Reservation, this legacy lives on to the present day.

Massachusetts's Biggest Cities

(Population numbers are from the US Census Bureau's 2017 projections for incorporated cities.)

1. Boston: population 685,094

Boston is the capital city of Massachusetts and its largest population hub. The city is located at the edge of the Charles River. Boston has an area of nearly 90 square miles (232 sq km), though nearly half is water. The city consists of twenty-three official neighborhoods.

Boston

2. Worcester: population 185,677

Located just 40 miles (64 km) west of Boston, Worcester is Massachusetts's second most populous city. Pronounced "WUS-tar," the city is located in the middle of the state and is thus known as the "Heart of the Commonwealth." According to legend, Valentine's cards were first mass-produced in this city.

3. Springfield: population 154,758

Springfield sits in western Massachusetts on the Connecticut River. The city is known as the "City of Firsts" due to the fact that many inventions were discovered here. Springfield's most famous "invention" is the game of basketball!

Cambridge

4. Cambridge: population 113,630

A city in its own right, Cambridge is often grouped with Boston. (Boston lies just south of Cambridge on the Charles River.) Cambridge is known for its innovation and education. The city is home to both Harvard University and Massachusetts Institute of Technology (MIT).

5. Lowell: population 111,346

Lowell is located on the Merrimack River. The city is home to the Lowell National Historical Park. Today, Lowell holds one of the largest populations of Cambodians in the country.

6. Brockton: population 95,672

Located approximately 25 miles (40 km) south of Boston, Brockton is often called the "City of Champions." The nickname is due to the many sports (and particularly boxing) champions born here, including Rocky Marciano.

7. New Bedford: population 95,120

Located on the south coast of Massachusetts, New Bedford was one of the most important whaling ports in the world during the nineteenth century. It is still known as "The Whaling City." Three islands on the Acushnet River form part of the city: Palmer's Island, Fish Island, and Pope's Island.

8. Quincy: population 94,166

Quincy is a suburb of Boston, located directly to the south of the city It is known as the "City of Presidents" because John Adams and John Quincy Adams were born there. John Hancock, the first signer of the Declaration of Independence, was also born in Quincy.

Newton

9. Lynn: population 94,063

A coastal city on the Atlantic Ocean, Lynn is 10 miles (16 km) north of downtown Boston. The city is the largest in Essex County. Lynn is home to one of the largest municipal parks in the country, the Lynn Woods Reservation.

10. Newton: population 88,994

Another suburb of Boston, Newton is located 7 miles (11 km) west of Boston. Newton is a popular city made up of thirteen villages. It's consistently ranked as one of the best cities in the country to live.

Cape Cod has dozens of beaches to choose from.

the glaciers drew back. Small rocks and giant boulders were left behind. The most famous of these boulders is Plymouth Rock.

Cape Cod

American writer Henry David Thoreau called Cape Cod "the bare and bended arm of Massachusetts." Cape Cod, located at the easternmost part of Massachusetts, stretches 65 miles (105 km) into the Atlantic Ocean. All along the cape, there are forests, swamps, salt marshes, sandy beaches, cliffs, and dunes. The outward side of the "arm" faces east to the Atlantic. Tides and storms pound the shoreline. A series of islands, including Nantucket, Martha's Vineyard, and the Elizabeth Islands, lie to the south in Nantucket Sound.

On the inside of the "arm's" curve, salt marshes and cranberry bogs line the shores of Cape Cod Bay.

Climate

It is not only the landscape in Massachusetts that offers a lot of variety. Residents of this New England state enjoy a full range of seasons— winter, spring, summer, and fall.

In summer, Massachusetts has consistent temperatures. Many summer days are humid

Fall in Carlisle

and sticky. In fall, days are cool and crisp, with clear blue skies. Leaves turn dazzling colors. When winter sets in, nights grow long, and the average temperature drops to 30 degrees Fahrenheit (–1 degree Celsius). Lakes and ponds freeze over, and snowfall can be as much as 67 inches (170 centimeters) a year in the colder mountainous areas. Spring is the shortest season. There may be frost on the ground as late as May.

Year-round, the ocean affects the climate along the coast. On a hot summer day, beachgoers enjoy cool breezes from the sea. In winter, coastal temperatures are usually warmer than inland. But nor'easters can roar across the North Atlantic Ocean and hit the beach with terrific force. Nor'easters blast coastal towns with heavy snowfalls and fallen trees, causing floods and power outages.

Wildlife and Water

Massachusetts features thousands of miles of seashore and riverbanks, as well as many wetlands, lakes, and ponds. Average rainfall in the state is 44 inches (112 cm), which is enough to keep most swamps, marshes, and rivers from going dry. These areas have long been home to a variety of Massachusetts's wildlife.

Since the 1860s, factories and towns have crowded the shores and riverbanks of the state's waterways. Waste from homes and factories has polluted rivers, lakes, streams, harbors, bays, and the ocean itself. Over time, many native species have died off completely. Others have become threatened or endangered. In 1988, President George H. W. Bush called Boston Harbor "the filthiest harbor in America." But Massachusetts residents took charge. After a multibillion-dollar

What Lives in Massachusetts?

Flora

A cranberry bog

Huckleberries

American Elms Also known as the white elm or water elm, the state tree of Massachusetts can reach 125 feet (38 m) in height. It can live in very cold conditions and has very hard wood. The Liberty Tree was an American elm in Boston that served as a rallying point during the lead-up to the American Revolution. In the middle of the twentieth century, a condition called Dutch elm disease killed millions of elms. Today, experts are planting more American elms in Massachusetts to help the trees bounce back.

Cranberries Cranberries are the fruit of shrubs or trailing vines that typically grow in bogs. They are related to huckleberries and are one of the United States' largest commercial crops. Cranberries have large amounts of vitamin C, fiber, and manganese. They are named as Massachusetts's state berry.

Huckleberries Huckleberries are the common name for several species of black and red berries that grow in Massachusetts and across New England. These berries were used by Native American populations to treat pain and infections. They are also common ingredients in pies and muffins. Animals and insects feast on this delicate and flavorful fruit.

Mayflowers Mayflowers' delicate light-pink blossoms prefer shady areas and sandy or rocky soil. The flower is found in every county in the state. Massachusetts schoolchildren chose the mayflower as the state's official flower in 1918.

White Oaks White oaks are common all along the northeastern coast of the United States. They can reach a height of 100 feet (30 m). It can take thirty years for a white oak to produce its first acorn! White oak trees in the United States have lived up to six hundred years.

White oak

Fauna

Beavers The beaver was an important animal for early colonists living in Massachusetts. At the time, beaver furs were an important **commodity** for trading. Years of trapping diminished the beaver population in the state from the early 1700s until the early 1900s. However, populations have been on the rise since the 1950s. This growth is due to a statewide effort to protect beavers.

Black-capped chickadee

Black-Capped Chickadee The black-capped chickadee is a small and curious bird. Its name refers to the black feathers that adorn its head. Chickadees are famous for their friendliness. They will often take advantage of bird feeders. In fact, chickadees have been known to take seeds directly from humans' hands.

Humpback Whale The endangered humpback whale brings many tourists to Massachusetts's shores. Humpback whales typically weigh in at 79,000 pounds (36,000 kilograms), making them one of the largest species of whales. There are only an estimated eighty thousand humpback whales in existence today.

Humpback whale

Snowy Tree Cricket The male snowy tree cricket is notable for its loud, melodious chirp. Known for their nearly white appearance, these crickets are actually living thermometers! Count the number of chirps you hear over a period of thirteen seconds and add forty to that number in order to calculate the current temperature in degrees Fahrenheit.

Spotted Salamander Renowned for its distinctive yellow spots, the spotted salamander typically lives in hardwood forests that have vernal, or spring, pools. While they are found all across the United States, the spotted salamander is especially protected in Massachusetts. There, state **environmentalists** have built special tunnels to help the salamanders safely cross under roadways.

Spotted salamander

cleanup effort, Boston Harbor is no longer a mess. The water is cleaner. Native fish species are back, and sea life is healthier. Swimmers, boaters, and beachcombers have returned. In fact, the Massachusetts federal court declared the three-decade-long cleanup to be completed—and a first-rate success—in the summer of 2016.

Today's citizens are also working to repair damage to the wild areas of Cape Cod. Early settlers, the Pilgrims, created Cape Cod's famous dunes when they cut down the trees for pastureland. Crashing waves and strong winds turned the treeless land into a sandy, desert-like place. At first, the sand was in danger of washing away. But beach grasses grew, holding the sand in place and protecting the habitats of the cape's creatures—red foxes, coyotes, great horned owls, marsh hawks, blue herons, hognose snakes, herring gulls, and piping plovers. Still, some beach dwellers continue to be at risk.

The US government lists the piping plover, a tiny bird, as threatened in Massachusetts. (People must take special steps to protect threatened or endangered plants and animals.) Cape Cod residents have closed off sections of beach where the plovers make their nests. Thanks to these efforts, the piping plover population is growing.

Another species at risk is the northern red-bellied cooter, formerly known as the Plymouth redbelly turtle. This

Cape Cod dunes

reptile has trouble sharing its home with human neighbors and is listed as an endangered species in Massachusetts. Redbellies live mainly in ponds but nest in forests and meadows. As human populations have increased, the turtles have lost protected nesting sites. The turtles' eggs—and tiny hatchlings—are especially vulnerable to predators such as skunks and raccoons. Predators destroy as many as half the cooters' nests each year.

These northern red-bellied cooters were part of a program designed to help hatchlings thrive.

In 1984, the Natural Heritage and Endangered Species Program (part of the Massachusetts Division of Fisheries and Wildlife) began a special effort to save the northern red-bellied cooter. Each fall, biologists collect about one hundred hatchlings from their nests. They raise the tiny baby turtles in captivity for the first year and then release the turtles into the wild. Thanks to this special treatment, the yearlings are the size of three-year-old turtles when they are set free. Large cooters are less likely to be preyed upon and have a better chance of surviving to adulthood. By 2016, more than four thousand red-bellied cooters had been released into the wild as part of the program.

As the history of the state shows, the people of Massachusetts have long valued their environment and the creatures they share it with. In fact, the state has long been associated with environmentalism and its focus on protecting the diversity of plants and animals living within its boundaries.

Wampanoag Native Americans meet with Plymouth colonists in the early 1600s.

2 The History of Massachusetts

Massachusetts has a long and rich history. In fact, the history of the area stretches back to prehistoric times. A lot has changed over time, from the landscape to who lives in what is now known as Massachusetts. However, some of Massachusetts's qualities have remained the same. This includes its importance. The state has consistently been a key player in shaping the history of the United States as a whole.

Early Inhabitants

The first people who lived in present-day Massachusetts arrived there about eleven thousand years ago. They made stone weapons for hunting and gathered nuts and berries from the forests and shellfish from the beaches. About two thousand to three thousand years ago, several Algonquian-speaking tribes settled along the streams and rivers of what is now Massachusetts.

Giovanni da Verrazzano explored the Atlantic coast.

They began to form semipermanent villages. The people lived in lodges and wigwams. They grew crops, hunted, and fished, moving with the seasons to take advantage of different food sources. Algonquian tribes living near the sea caught fish and hunted whales. Those living on Cape Cod were called the Nauset. Other Algonquians were the Patuxet, Wampanoag, and Nipmuc tribes.

Explorers and Colonists

Historians believe that about a thousand years ago, Norse explorers might have been the first Europeans to view the lands that would become Massachusetts. About five hundred years went by before other European explorers reached what is now New England. The Italian explorer Giovanni da Verrazzano **surveyed** the northeast coast of North America in 1524. In the next century, John Smith (who had founded the Jamestown colony in Virginia in 1607) gave New England its name. He mapped the area from Penobscot Bay, in present-day Maine, to Cape Cod in 1614.

During the early 1600s, unrest was growing in England. The Church of England had become very powerful and forbade people to practice other religions. Some people opposed to the Church of England became known as Separatists. Some of them decided to leave.

On September 16, 1620, a group of 102 Separatists (now known as Pilgrims) and other English people set sail for America aboard a ship named the *Mayflower*. The two-month sea journey was horrid. The Pilgrims had been granted territory in Virginia, but the *Mayflower* strayed off course. The newcomers came ashore at Cape Cod. After attempts to reach a destination in New York failed, they decided to stay near where they first landed. They wrote an agreement called the Mayflower Compact. In it, they promised to govern themselves and to make only fair and just laws "for ye generall good of ye Colonie."

The first Pilgrim settlement was a coastal village they called Plimoth (spelled Plymouth today). The Pilgrims knew that a cold winter would soon be upon them. Therefore, they quickly built homes using poles and grasses. Wild animals lurked in the woods. The Native people made the Pilgrims uneasy. Yet the Pilgrims were pleasantly

The *Mayflower* began its voyage to America in 1620.

Native Americans in Massachusetts

Many people lived in Massachusetts before the first European settlers arrived. These people were the Natives of Massachusetts. The eastern section of the state, including the Atlantic coastal portions of the land, was settled by the Wampanoag people. Other eastern tribes of Massachusetts included the Massachuset, the Nantucket, the Nauset, and the Pennacook. The central portion of the state was settled by the Mohegan, Nipmuc, and Pequot tribes.

Wampanoag wigwams are sometimes called *wetus*.

The Mohican tribe, as well as the Pocomtuc, were located in the western portion of what is now Massachusetts.

Most of the Native tribes of the Massachusetts region raised their own food through farming. Corn, squash, and beans were common crops. The men also hunted deer, turkeys, and small game to supplement their meals. The people that lived on the ocean's coast fished as well. Most of the Native people of Massachusetts lived in wigwams, small rounded houses constructed with wooden frames covered with birch bark. Another name for wigwam was *wetu*, the Wampanoag term for "house."

As the Europeans settled in the Massachusetts colony, they made contact with more local tribes in an attempt to convert the Natives to Christianity. This contact had deadly consequences. The Europeans introduced diseases that the Natives had never been exposed to before. These illnesses wiped out significant portions of the Native population. In order to survive, many of the tribes merged together. However, these combinations led to a loss of tribal distinctions. Traditions were lost over time. Distinct languages merged into a single way of speaking.

Today there are two federally recognized Native tribes in Massachusetts—the Mashpee Wampanoag Indian Tribal Council and the Wampanoag Tribe of Gay Head (Aquinnah) of Massachusetts. The **state** itself recognizes the Nipmuc Nation as well.

Spotlight on the Wampanoag

"Wampanoag" means "easterners." In the 1600s, there were more than ten thousand Wampanoag people in dozens of villages along the coast of Massachusetts. Today, a few thousand Wampanoag people live in New England. There is a reservation for the tribe on Martha's Vineyard.

Organization: The Wampanoag were organized into a confederation. The leader was called a sachem, who led over other lower-level sachems within the organization. Both women and men could be sachems.

Clothing: The Wampanoag wore breechcloths, which were made from deerskin. Women often wore deerskin skirts tied with thin belts. Both men and women wore leggings to protect their legs. Men's leggings were longer, and they were tied at the waist.

Children: Young Wampanoag boys learned to gather, hunt, and fish from their parents. Young girls learned how to make clothing, plant crops, and collect food. Both girls and boys were taught how to work together as a community. They also learned from their elders through the stories that they told.

Games: One game the Wampanoag played was called "the bowl game" or "hubbub." It consisted of a wooden bowl and flat, marked playing pieces. One side of these pieces was dark and the other side was light. The players bounced the playing pieces by bumping the bowl. They kept score using sticks that were passed back and forth, depending on who won each toss. As the players bounced the pieces, they said, "hub, hub, hub."

This illustration shows Squanto helping the Pilgrims survive their first year in America.

surprised to find fields ready for planting. It gave them hope for spring.

The Wampanoag tribe and their chief, Massasoit, watched the newcomers carefully. Finally, the chief sent a messenger named Samoset, who arrived at Plymouth and said simply, "Welcome, English." (Samoset had probably learned some of the language from Englishmen who came to fish off the coast of what is now northern New England and Canada.) The Pilgrims were excited to find someone who spoke their language. They eagerly began to ask him questions. The Pilgrims wondered why there were fields ready for planting but no people in the area. Samoset told them the tilled fields belonged to the Patuxet, a tribe whose members had all died from disease. After Samoset brought his report back to Massasoit, the chief and his attendants visited Plymouth. Though there was little trust between the two groups, the Wampanoag tribe and the Pilgrims signed the first peace treaty between Europeans and Native Americans. It lasted for more than fifty years.

One member of Chief Massasoit's party was a man named Tisquantum, or Squanto. He was the last remaining Patuxet. He spoke English because he had once lived in England as a slave. Squanto wanted to live on his ancestors' land and decided to help the Pilgrims. He taught them how to grow corn, where to hunt and fish, and which berries and nuts were good to eat. Thanks to Squanto, the Pilgrims were able to survive their first year in the new land and harvest a crop. For three days after the harvest, the Pilgrims and Massasoit's tribe celebrated an English feast called Harvest Home, which Americans now call Thanksgiving.

In the following years, the Pilgrims' colony grew in size as more people came from England and several new towns were established.

The Puritans

In 1628, the first members of another religious group—the Puritans—arrived in the area. They joined an existing small settlement that was later named Salem. In 1630, a much larger group of Puritans arrived and soon settled nearby in what is now Boston to establish the Massachusetts Bay Colony.

The Puritans built small villages surrounding a section of open land called a commons. They farmed nearby fields in warm weather and made useful things, such as furniture, farm tools, horse harnesses, and clothing, in winter. The Puritans were stern people who believed in simple living and hard work.

New settlers continued to arrive from England, and the Massachusetts settlements grew. In 1691, England combined the Plymouth and Massachusetts Bay Colonies into the single colony of Massachusetts.

A girl faints while accusing a woman of witchcraft in a Salem courtroom.

"Witchcraft" in Salem

In many ways, life was difficult in seventeenth-century Massachusetts. The Puritans were powerful and often forced their beliefs on others. Puritan farmers and Native Americans fought bitterly over land. Many colony members did not trust one another. In 1692, when two girls in Salem fell sick seemingly without cause, the so-called Dark Days began. The girls fainted, had seizures, and slept little. A doctor declared them bewitched, a condition punishable by hanging. The girls blamed a slave named Tituba, saying, "She afflicts me! She comes to me at night and torments me! She's a witch!"

Soon, people all over Salem were accusing each other of witchcraft. Most of the accused were unmarried or widowed women who owned farmland. Many historians think that the accusers wanted the women's property. A court was set up to hear the witchcraft cases. In less than a year, more than 150 people were sent to prison. By the time the "Witchcraft Court" was shut down, 20 people had been executed.

The Salem witchcraft trials marked a troubled time in Massachusetts's history, as did the struggle over land between the Native Americans and the English colonists. In 1675, Massasoit's son, Metacom, declared war after the colonists executed three tribesman. After two years of brutal fighting, King Philip (as Metacom was known by colonists) was killed in battle. Many of his Native American supporters fled to

Canada or westward. Others stayed and adopted English ways.

King Philip's War, as it was called, was not the only land conflict the colonists—or the English—faced in America. Fur traders and settlers from France had also come to eastern North America. In the 1600s and 1700s, France and Great Britain fought several wars for control of eastern North America and its valuable natural resources. The French and Indian War (1754–1763) was the largest of these conflicts. Great Britain won the war. However, the victory came at a great price. The British government had borrowed a great deal of money to pay for the war.

A Demand for Representation

To help raise money to pay off the country's debt, King George III and the British Parliament began imposing new taxes on the colonies. The king was also eager to regain control over colonial governments that had been acting more and more independently while Britain was distracted by its wars. The British government wanted its American colonies to trade only with Britain. On the other hand, many people in Massachusetts wanted to be free to trade with other countries too.

Several new taxes and other actions by the British government, starting in 1763, angered the colonists. When the first of the Townshend Acts was passed in 1767, many colonists had had enough. The Townshend Acts put new taxes on many kinds of imported goods. Many colonists did not feel they should have to pay taxes imposed by a government in which they had no voice. Colonists who opposed the actions

The Boston Massacre claimed five people's lives.

Protesters held the Boston Tea Party in 1773.

of the British government became known as patriots. Their battle cry became, "No taxation without representation!"

The idea for independence had been planted. Then, on March 5, 1770, British soldiers opened fire on colonial protesters in an attack later known as the Boston Massacre. Five people were killed. Later, many colonists opposed the British government's tax on tea. A group called the Sons of Liberty organized a protest called the Boston Tea Party. One night in 1773, the protesters sneaked aboard a ship full of English tea in Boston Harbor and threw the tea overboard. In 1774, the British government passed a series of laws that became known in the colonies as the Intolerable Acts. One of the measures was to close the port of Boston.

Soon British soldiers, or "regulars," wearing red coats were everywhere. Farmers put down their plows for guns. They called themselves "minutemen" because it was said they could prepare for battle in just one minute. British soldiers planned to march on the towns of Lexington and Concord (outside Boston) to capture patriot leaders and seize weapons. A group of patriots discovered their plan. Boston silversmith Paul Revere secretly rowed across the Charles River. He and two other men then journeyed on horseback through the countryside to warn the minutemen that the British were coming.

A Revolution Begins

On April 19, 1775, minutemen and British regulars confronted each other at Lexington. The first fighting of the American Revolution took place there. (It is not known for certain who fired the first shot—what poet Ralph Waldo Emerson later called "the shot heard round the world.")

From Lexington, the British went on to Concord. There they battled again with minutemen. As the British retreated back to Boston, colonial forces repeatedly shot at them. At the end of the day's fighting, some 250 British soldiers were dead or wounded. About 90 Americans had been killed or injured. The military consequences were not great, but the outcome gave the colonists hope. They had managed to embarrass the better equipped, better trained—and more respected—British army.

Lexington and Concord were the first battles of the American Revolution. Today, a monument to the battles stands in Lexington.

After the battles of Lexington and Concord, the British soldiers stayed in Boston. Reinforcements arrived in May. In June, American forces were sent to Charlestown Peninsula, across the Charles River from Boston, to occupy Bunker Hill. They ended up building fortifications on nearby Breed's Hill. British soldiers tried to storm the fortifications and were pushed back twice, suffering heavy losses. The American forces, low on **ammunition**, fled when the British regulars made their third charge.

More than 1,000 British troops and 450 Americans were killed or wounded during the Battle of Bunker Hill. Although the colonists had been pushed back, they still encircled the British in Boston. Months later, in March 1776, General George Washington's forces occupied Dorchester Heights, a line of hills south of Boston that overlooked the city. Washington's men placed cannons there. British general William Howe soon realized he was in the middle of enemy territory occupying a city that he could

Bunker Hill Day

Every year on June 17, many residents of Massachusetts celebrate Bunker Hill Day. Bunker Hill was a battle that the American army actually lost against British troops. It seems unlikely, then, that this would be a day for celebration. Yet the Battle of Bunker Hill was both the first major battle of the war and a turning point in the American Revolution. It showed the American people that their militias could inflict great damage on the more organized and better-trained British troops.

On June 17, 1775, British troops stationed around Charlestown became aware of the presence of the American militia nearby. They attacked the American troops throughout the day. Eventually, the American militia was forced out of Charlestown. The British retook control of the area, although they suffered 1,054 **casualties**. The American militia suffered 450 casualties in all. Bolstered by this battle, American troops and their supporters grew more confident as they entered into battles. They used retreat as a sound strategy throughout the remainder of the Revolutionary War. To commemorate this momentous battle, Americans first began celebrating June 17 in 1786.

Today, Bunker Hill Day is celebrated in Suffolk County and areas of Middlesex County, in Massachusetts, including the city of Boston. Generally, the holiday is celebrated with a parade that circles around most of Charlestown, featuring a Revolutionary War band and other period actors. A battle reenactment is also a part of the festivities. The reenactment attracts many families from the Boston area and beyond.

But tourists who are interested in the Revolutionary War can also visit the Bunker Hill Monument at any time. This 221-foot (67.4 m) granite monument was built to commemorate the battle between 1825 and 1843. It is one of the most visible landmarks in the Boston area.

The Battle of Bunker Hill took place on June 17, 1775. Since 1786, areas of Massachusetts have commemorated the battle.

not defend. On March 17, 1776, the British army left Boston for good.

Independence!

A few months later, on July 4, 1776, the **Second Continental Congress** adopted the Declaration of Independence. Of course, declaring independence

The signing of the Declaration of Independence

does not make it so. For the next seven years, the colonists continued to battle British soldiers throughout the thirteen colonies. The Treaty of Paris ended the war in 1783, with Great Britain recognizing American independence. It is estimated that more than twenty-five thousand American soldiers had died for the cause.

In Massachusetts, John Adams and other leaders wrote a constitution for the Commonwealth of Massachusetts. (The first draft was called a Constitution for the State of Massachusetts, but people rejected it.) The document included rules for a new government that was based on **democracy** and citizens' rights. It did not include rights for women and slaves. It was a model for the US Constitution and the Bill of Rights. In 1788, Massachusetts became the sixth state to ratify the US Constitution.

Another Kind of Revolution

In the nineteenth century, Massachusetts played a major role in another revolution—the Industrial Revolution. There had been manufacturing in Massachusetts since the mid-1600s. Yet the state did not become a powerhouse in the industry

Make Your Own Revolutionary Printing Press

One of the reasons why the revolutionary spirit spread so quickly across the American colonies was the spread of political pamphlets. These pamphlets were short, printed documents that often stoked American anger against the British. But pamphlets could not be made without a printing press. Therefore, many historians have said the availability of the printing press was a big factor in the success of the American Revolution. Here is a simple way you can make your own pamphlet or Revolutionary War lithograph using only Styrofoam, paper, a rolling pin, and paint or ink.

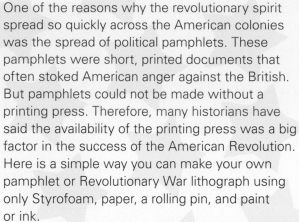

Supplies

- A flat piece of Styrofoam (you can cut out the bottom of a Styrofoam takeout container)
- A pen or pencil
- Several sheets of paper
- A rolling pin
- A foam brush
- Paint (such as tempura) or ink

Directions

1. Use a pen or pencil to carve out images or letters on the Styrofoam. Remember that they should be written backwards for them to read correctly on your pamphlet.
2. Using a foam brush, evenly coat your carved Styrofoam with paint or ink.
3. Place the carved Styrofoam facedown on a blank piece of paper.
4. Making sure not to move the Styrofoam, firmly roll the rolling pin over it several times.
5. Peel off the Styrofoam to reveal your printed pamphlet. Now, you can repeat the steps again to make more pamphlets for distribution!

Two factory workers use Francis Cabot Lowell's water-powered loom in the 1850s.

until about two hundred years later. In 1814, a Massachusetts resident named Francis Cabot Lowell built a loom in Waltham that ran by waterpower. A loom is a device that weaves thread into cloth. Lowell had visited a cotton mill in England, where he closely examined the workings of a power loom. Before he built his first mill with a water-powered loom, American looms were operated by hand. A water-powered loom can weave cloth much more quickly than a hand-operated one. Another one of Lowell's mills transformed the town of Lowell into the nation's first major manufacturing city. The Industrial Revolution had come to Massachusetts.

Cities such as Lawrence, Fall River, and New Bedford soon had large factories for making textiles (cloth), taking advantage of the waterpower in the state's rivers. By the end of the nineteenth century, Massachusetts produced more than a third of the nation's wool and cotton cloth. In Dalton, the Crane Paper Company produced the special paper used to make the nation's money. Factories in Lynn, Worcester, and

FAST FACT

Basketball was invented in Springfield, Massachusetts, by Dr. James Naismith. Naismith was a professor at what is known as Springfield College today. The first basketball game was played to keep his gym class busy during a rainy day in 1891.

Marlborough made shoes and boots for the entire country. Many factory employees were women and children who worked long hours in difficult conditions for very little pay.

Wars and Recovery

Industrialized states in the North contrasted with those in the South. In the South, agriculture was the main industry. Another issue, slavery, eventually divided the two regions even further. On the plantations of the South, most of the hard labor was done by African American slaves.

Massachusetts was the first slaveholding New England colony and played a role in what's known as the triangular trade. Triangular trade involved enslaving Africans, selling them, and using that revenue to buy products like sugar. The route of trade forms a triangle on a map. Slavery came to an end in Massachusetts in the 1780s and gradually ended in other Northern states as well. Like other Northern states, Massachusetts had an abolitionist (or antislavery) movement, dedicated to ending slavery nationwide. Many people say the movement began in 1831. That's when William Lloyd Garrison first published his antislavery newspaper, the *Liberator*, in Boston. Eventually, the differences between North and South led eleven Southern states to secede (withdraw) from the United States. The Civil War (1861–1865) was fought to keep the nation together.

William Lloyd Garrison published an important antislavery newspaper in Boston.

When the Civil War broke out, Massachusetts quickly answered President Abraham Lincoln's call to arms. The state sent the first troops into battle. Military units from Massachusetts included the Fifty-Fourth Massachusetts Regiment, one of the first African American regiments in the country. Those who remained at home went to work in factories making guns, ammunition, ships, tents, blankets, and bandages. After the South was defeated and the Civil War ended, the Thirteenth Amendment to the US Constitution abolished slavery throughout the United States.

A memorial to the Fifty-Fourth Massachusetts Regiment

In the 1840s, thousands of immigrants came to Massachusetts to escape a severe **famine** in Ireland. In the later decades of the nineteenth century, people from many different countries poured into Massachusetts looking for work. Immigrants from France, Italy, Poland, Ireland, Portugal, Germany, and Greece joined immigrants from Finland, Latvia, Lithuania, and Turkey in seeking a better life in the commonwealth. Many of these workers had valuable skills. Because of them, Massachusetts prospered. This era of progress, known as the Industrial Age, lasted through the outbreak of World War I.

When America entered World War I in 1917, many Massachusetts citizens enlisted to fight for their country. Others stayed at home, building guns and ships and manufacturing other supplies. After the war ended, telephones, automobiles, electricity, and other new conveniences rapidly improved daily life.

Then, in 1929, the stock market crashed and everything changed. During the period known as the Great Depression, people lost their jobs, businesses closed, and banks failed. Few people escaped hardship. The federal government took many steps to strengthen the economy. In time, things began to turn around. When World War II broke out in Europe in 1939, once again Massachusetts's skilled workers were needed. By 1941, the United States had entered the war. Massachusetts's factories were busy producing wartime goods.

After the end of World War II in 1945, Massachusetts continued to be an important site of recovery and economic growth. Boston developed into an international city where workers from all over could find new jobs in finance, medicine, and technology.

A State of Big Ideas

After World War II, innovators in Massachusetts continued to change the world. In 1947, inventor Percy Spencer unveiled the microwave oven, which he created in the state. In 1954, Massachusetts surgeons completed the first successful kidney transplant. A computer programmer sent the world's first email from Massachusetts in 1971. These are just a few examples of how Massachusetts residents have always had big, important ideas. Modern-day Massachusetts is no exception.

In 2007, a recession hit the United States. A recession is when the economy declines instead of staying the same or growing. Recessions can lead to people losing their jobs and their houses. Creative thinking and hard work in Massachusetts meant that the state recovered fast. The *Boston Globe* reported in 2010 that "Massachusetts appeared to weather the recession better than other states last year." The recession officially ended in 2009.

But the economy is not the only place where Massachusetts's big ideas pay off. The research universities in the state lead to the development of some truly awesome progress.

As of 2018, Harvard and the Massachusetts Institute of Technology are two of the universities with the most Nobel Prize winners in the world.

Thanks to the innovation that Massachusetts is known for, the country looks to it as a leader. In 2006, then-governor Mitt Romney created a health-care plan for Massachusetts. The plan provides coverage for everyone living in the state. The lawmakers who created the Affordable Care Act in 2009 (also known as Obamacare) used Romney's plan as a template.

With so many fresh ideas, Massachusetts's future looks bright.

Governor Mitt Romney signed a new Massachusetts health-care plan into law in 2006.

Massachusetts's Important People

John Quincy Adams

John Quincy Adams

The son of president John Adams, John Quincy Adams also became a US president. In addition, he worked as a US diplomat, senator, and member of the House of Representatives for Massachusetts. Born in Quincy, where his father was also born and raised, Adams became a vocal critic of slavery and was influential in shaping United States foreign policy.

Susan B. Anthony

Susan B. Anthony was born in Adams, although she moved to Rochester, New York, as a child. Anthony was an abolitionist and women's **suffrage** activist. Along with Elizabeth Cady Stanton, Anthony founded the National Woman Suffrage Association. Her work eventually led to the passage of the Nineteenth Amendment, which granted women the right to vote in the United States.

Clara Barton

Clara Barton

Clara Barton was born in North Oxford in 1821. She became one of the world's most famous nurses and eventually founded the American Red Cross. Despite not having any formal training, Barton began nursing injured soldiers during the Civil War. Her courageousness on the battlefield made her famous as the "Angel of the Battlefield."

Emily Dickinson

Emily Dickinson is perhaps one of the most famous poets in American history. Born in Amherst in 1830, Dickinson was famously shy. She rarely left her hometown. Later, she rarely left her house. Publishing only some poems during her lifetime, she did not achieve fame until after her death. Dickinson's home is now a popular museum dedicated to her life and work.

W. E. B. Du Bois

W. E. B. Du Bois was born in Great Barrington, Massachusetts, in 1868. Du Bois spent his life working to secure rights for African Americans. He was an author, activist, historian, and one of the founders of the National Association for the Advancement of Colored People (NAACP). In 1895, Du Bois became the first African American to earn a PhD from Harvard University.

Emily Dickinson

Ralph Waldo Emerson

A famous essayist and poet, Ralph Waldo Emerson founded the transcendentalist movement in the United States. Born in Boston in 1803, Emerson's transcendental philosophy focused on nature, freedom, and the role of the individual in society. He became an important mentor to another famous Massachusetts resident: Henry David Thoreau.

Robert Lowell

Born to an elite Boston family that could trace its heritage back to the *Mayflower*, Robert Lowell became an important poet. Boston was often the setting for his poetry. In 1947, Lowell was named the sixth poet laureate consultant in poetry to the Library of Congress. He also won the Pulitzer Prize for Poetry in both 1947 and 1974.

Robert Lowell

Phillis Wheatley

Phillis Wheatley was born in West Africa in 1753. As a young girl, she was sold into slavery, and she ended up in Boston. The family who bought her taught her to read and write. Wheatley was an extremely talented poet. In fact, she became the first African American to publish a book of poetry. Wheatley was freed from slavery in 1773 and died in 1784. After her death, two more books of her writing were published.

More than half of all Massachusetts residents live within 50 miles (80 km) of Boston.

3 Who Lives in Massachusetts?

Some Massachusetts residents are able to trace their family history in the state over hundreds of years. Yet that's not the full picture of who lives in the state. Many more people have come to the state from all over the world in recent decades.

Massachusetts ranks forty-fifth among the states in size, but as of 2017, it ranked fifteenth in population. Only two states—New Jersey and Rhode Island—have denser populations. (Population density refers to the number of people per square mile or square kilometer.) Today, more than half of all Bay Staters live in towns, cities, and suburbs within 50 miles (80 km) of Boston.

According to 2016 US census estimates, 73 percent of people living in Massachusetts identify as white, 8.6 percent are African American, 6.7 percent are Asian, and 11.5 percent are Hispanic/Latino. Census estimates put the Native American population at 0.5 percent of the total population.

FAST FACT

Massachusetts is one of only a handful of states to have its own state polka: "Say Hello to Someone from Massachusetts" by Lenny Gomulka. Its lyrics include: "Say hello to someone in Massachusetts, / Tip your hat to every lady that you meet, / Shake a hand, you'll make a friend in Massachusetts, / That New England old-time custom can't be beat."

Irish people gather seaweed to eat during the potato famine.

A Cultural Melting Pot

After the Native American population shrank in the 1600s and 1700s, English settlers became the most powerful group in Massachusetts. For centuries, the families who traced their beginnings in America to the *Mayflower* dominated the culture of the commonwealth. (These families include the Cabot, Lodge, Adams, Emerson, and Lowell families.) For the most part, this hardworking, reserved group of people—sometimes called Yankees—represented the Massachusetts way of life to the world.

Then, in the 1840s, Irish immigrants came in great numbers to escape Ireland's potato famine. The Yankees felt threatened by the Irish immigrants and tried to keep them from going to public events. They even posted "No Irish Need Apply" signs to keep the new arrivals from getting jobs. Today, however, Irish Americans are the state's largest ethnic group and are very active in the state's politics, society, and trade.

After the Irish came ashore, people from Germany, Russia, Poland, Portugal, Italy, Greece, and French Canada immigrated to Massachusetts. These eager newcomers settled in the many mill and factory towns and began building communities.

After the European cultures created a flavorful blend of traditions, a new ingredient was added. Since the 1970s, immigrants from Latin America, the Caribbean, and Asia have settled in Lowell and other cities. Often, children playing in neighborhood parks speak English to one another while at night they speak Khmer

FAST FACT

The first practical sewing machine was invented by Elias Howe in Boston in 1845. Over his lifetime, Howe earned the equivalent of $5 million in sales of this new, popular machine.

Population Shifts

Although Massachusetts is the sixth-smallest state in the United States, it is the third most densely populated area in the country. The state's population is edging toward seven million residents. In fact, Massachusetts has experienced the largest population growth in the Northeast. In previous years, the largest growth occurred in the capital city of Boston. Today, there is major growth outside the big cities. The reason for this increase in population is simple: increased immigration. In modern times, about 15 percent of Bay Staters have come to Massachusetts from outside of the United States.

More than fifty years ago, the town of Quincy had only one hundred residents with Asian heritage as part of its population. As of 2016, that number increased to 23,986. This means Asian Americans make up over a quarter of the population. Quincy actually has a larger percent of immigrant residents than Boston. Quincy beats out the capital by 2 percentage points at 29 percent. City officials expect Asian immigrants to make up 30 percent of Quincy's population by 2020. Most immigrants arrive from China, followed by Vietnam and India.

Population shifts like the one in Quincy mean that new cultural traditions and languages are becoming influential in these regions. Newspapers such as the *Patriot Ledger*, based in Quincy, offer some of their articles in Chinese. Translations of school board meetings are provided in Mandarin. Many more language classes are also being offered at local schools.

As Massachusetts is becoming increasingly diverse, it is becoming more important to offer students new cultural experiences. Today, children in schools across the state are offered language classes such as Portuguese, Spanish, Cantonese and Mandarin Chinese, and Vietnamese. A growing percentage of children over the age of five in the state are bilingual and speak another language at home besides English. This diversity has enriched Massachusetts's culture and has made it one of the most popular (and populous!) states in the nation.

Some newspapers in Quincy print articles in Chinese to cater to the city's large population of Chinese speakers.

A Cambodian restaurant in Lowell

(the language of Cambodia) or Spanish to family members at home. Lowell's Cambodian community is the second largest in the nation.

Many of Boston's neighborhoods have a lively ethnic and cultural atmosphere. Its oldest neighborhood, the North End, has a particularly rich immigrant history. Its narrow streets were laid out in the 1600s along the city's **wharves**. When immigrants stepped off their ships, they found it easy to move into the buildings nearby. English, Polish, Russian, Jewish, Portuguese, Irish, and Italian immigrants all made homes in this historic community. Today, the neighborhood is mostly Italian. Hispanics from the Dominican Republic, Puerto Rico, Cuba, and many other Spanish-speaking areas have contributed to the blend of cultures in neighborhoods south of Boston.

Another lively neighborhood full of shops, businesses, and restaurants is Chinatown. Many people of Chinese, Japanese, Korean, Cambodian, and Vietnamese descent live and work there.

The Massachusetts Institute of Technology is world famous.

A Culture of Learning

Higher education has been important to Massachusetts since the 1600s. Harvard University was founded in 1636. It was the first institution of higher learning in what would become the United States. Later, in the nineteenth century, many other major

Why is this famous dish associated with Boston? Because Boston has long been a hub for molasses. Molasses is essential to the original recipe, which dates back to colonial times.

Boston Baked Beans

Ingredients

- 1 pound navy beans
- 1/2 pound chopped bacon
- 1/3 cup molasses
- 1/3 cup brown sugar
- 4 tablespoons Dijon mustard
- 1/8 teaspoon ground cloves
- 1 medium onion, chopped
- 3 cups hot water

Directions

1. Cover beans with water and bring to a boil. Then remove them from the heat.
2. Let the beans sit for one hour before draining.
3. Preheat oven to 325 degrees Fahrenheit.
4. Mix molasses, sugar, mustard, and cloves with the three cups of hot water.
5. In a Dutch oven, cook bacon over a medium flame until it is lightly brown. Add onions and cook until you can smell them.
6. Add beans to the Dutch oven and stir.
7. Add molasses mixture to the beans in the Dutch oven and combine. Bring to a simmer.
8. Transfer the Dutch oven to the oven and bake, uncovered, for four hours or until the beans are soft but mostly still whole.
9. Stir beans. Their consistency should be thick and glazed.
10. Add salt and pepper to taste, and enjoy!

Massachusetts's Biggest Colleges and Universities

(All enrollment numbers are from US News and World Report 2018 college rankings.)

University of Massachusetts Amherst

Boston University

Boston College

Harvard University

1. University of Massachusetts Amherst

(23,373 undergraduate students)

2. Boston University

(17,944 undergraduate students)

3. University of Massachusetts Lowell

(13,639 undergraduate students)

4. Northeastern University, Boston

(13,473 undergraduate students)

5. University of Massachusetts Boston

(12,847 undergraduate students)

6. Bridgewater State University

(9,562 undergraduate students)

7. Boston College

(9,309 undergraduate students)

8. Salem State University

(7,346 undergraduate students)

9. University of Massachusetts Dartmouth

(6,999 undergraduate students)

10. Harvard University, Cambridge

(6,710 undergraduate students)

colleges and universities were established in Massachusetts. In or near the capital city are Boston University, Brandeis University, Northeastern University, Boston College, and the Massachusetts Institute of Technology. Farther west are Williams College, Clark University, Amherst College, the University of Massachusetts, and the Worcester Polytechnic Institute. Traditional women's colleges such as Radcliffe (now part of Harvard), Smith, Mount Holyoke, and Wellesley were founded in the late nineteenth century (and some now offer coed programs). Because many Massachusetts residents are so well educated, the Bay State has long been at the leading edge of ideas and achievements.

Massachusetts was the first state in the nation to require all children to attend public school. However, not all schools were equal. Throughout most of the country's history, many schools in the United States were **segregated**. White children and black children went to different schools.

In many Southern states, laws and government policies established totally separate school systems for white children and black children. In many states, including Massachusetts, this was not the case. However, African American families in Massachusetts tended to live in different neighborhoods. Therefore, their children went to different schools. The schools for African American children often had inferior facilities and out-of-date textbooks. In 1954, a case called *Brown v. Board of Education of Topeka, Kansas* changed everything. The US Supreme Court ruled that segregated schools violated the US Constitution. Still, many states were slow to integrate their school systems.

In 1965, more than ten years after the *Brown* ruling, Boston schools were still largely

John D. O'Bryant (*left*) was the first African American member of the Boston School Committee. Here, he stands with other committee members and the superintendent in 1978.

segregated. Schools in black neighborhoods tended to be inferior to those in white areas of the city. With the help of the National Association for the Advancement of Colored People (NAACP), black parents complained to the Boston School **Committee**. However, Louise Hicks, the committee chair, claimed the black schools were not inferior. "A racially imbalanced school," she said, "is not educationally harmful."

After years of trying to change the situation, black parents in Boston finally took their case to court. In 1974, a federal district court judge ordered the schools to integrate. To achieve a balance of black students and white students, children were bused to schools in different parts of the city. Many white people opposed the new busing policy. In September, buses carrying black students in South Boston were met by angry mobs throwing rocks. Some white parents even pulled their children out of school. The resistance to busing and the violent behavior continued for years. The situation finally settled down after Hicks was replaced as committee chair and

John D. O'Bryant, an African American man, was elected to the committee.

Today, approximately 3,300 students currently participate in the program that buses students across Boston. It is called METCO. About 10,000 students are on a waiting list, hoping they will have the chance to get a quality education. There are many critics of the program who believe that money should go to improving inner-city schools in Boston rather than to the METCO program. Yet there are also many advocates for the program—including students who have participated in it. "At first I didn't like [the school I was bused to]," said one METCO student. "But as I got older, I realized the difference between the schools and the opportunities I got." Indeed, inner-city students in METCO programs are more likely to graduate from high school than their peers. Around 94 percent of METCO students graduate from high school, a larger number than the state average.

As Massachusetts becomes more diverse, the state government will need to determine how to create opportunities for all residents, no matter their race, religion, or country of origin. Programs like METCO are a great start.

These students are part of the METCO program, which buses students across Boston.

Massachusetts's Celebrities

Steve Carell

John Cena

Steve Carell

Actor Steve Carell is known for his slapstick humor and his gentle characters. Born in Concord, Massachusetts, Carell has been nominated for the Academy Award for Best Actor and the Golden Globe Award for Best Actor. He was also named "America's funniest man" by *Life* magazine.

John Cena

Born in West Newbury, Massachusetts, John Cena is perhaps the most recognizable face of professional wrestling. Throughout his WWE career, Cena has won sixteen world championships and is a five-time United States champion. Cena is also known for his volunteer work. He has granted the most wishes of any celebrity at the Make-A-Wish Foundation.

Mindy Kaling

A native of Cambridge and a graduate of Dartmouth College, Mindy Kaling shot to fame during her time on the comedy series *The Office*. She has since written two best-selling memoirs.

Conan O'Brien

A star of late night comedy, Conan O'Brien was born and raised in the Boston suburb of Brookline. O'Brien attended Harvard University before breaking out in comedy. At Harvard, he was president of the comedy magazine the *Harvard Lampoon*.

Mindy Kaling

Amy Poehler

Born in Newton, Massachusetts, Amy Poehler is an actress, comedian, director, and writer. She has starred in the series *Parks and Recreation* and *Saturday Night Live* and has provided her voice for blockbuster animated films like *Inside Out* and *Horton Hears a Who!*

Aly Raisman

As a gold-medal Olympic gymnast, Aly Raisman has earned many accolades. Born in Needham, Massachusetts, the star has traveled the world performing her sport but always receives a big welcome when returning home.

Aly Raisman

Whaling was big business for Massachusetts in the 1700s and 1800s. Today, whale-watching brings tourists to the state.

4 At Work in Massachusetts

The technology sector drives Massachusetts's economy today, as well as the service and tourism industries. New and exciting technology start-ups are now providing employment opportunities and making Massachusetts a state that always remains on the edge of innovation.

Agricultural Endeavors

In the late 1700s and early 1800s, fishing and whaling contributed greatly to the state's pocketbook. When the New Bedford whaling boom reached its peak in 1857, more than three hundred vessels were sailing out of the port. The fleet, worth more than $12 million, employed ten thousand men. By the early 1900s, however, the whaling industry in America was virtually dead. Today, whale populations off the coast of Massachusetts contribute to the state economy in a much more humane way.

FAST FACT

The first chocolate factory in the United States was built in Dorchester, Massachusetts. Dr. James Baker and John Hannon teamed up to make the first chocolate business in the late eighteenth century. They built a successful company based in Dorchester that lasted generations. In 1995, the Baker Chocolate Company was sold to Kraft Foods.

These fishermen are sorting cod and haddock in Chatham.

According to the World Wildlife Fund, the Bay State is one of the top-ten whale-watching spots in the world.

New England's fishing industry has always been tied to groundfishing, or catching bottom-dwelling fish such as cod and haddock. The 1970s saw a decline in the industry due to overfishing and pollution. The state has made a comeback, though. The economic impact of Massachusetts's fishing industry is one of the top in the country.

Workers harvest cranberries in Halifax

Although fewer Bay Staters work in farming than any other industry, Massachusetts is still home to thousands of farms. As of 2015, the value of agricultural production—crop and livestock sales—was $492 million on average each year. In southeastern Massachusetts, farmers grow about 26 percent of the country's cranberry crop. The tart red berry is a Native American fruit. Algonquian tribes used it for food and medicine and as a dye for blankets and rugs.

Developing Products and Ideas

After Francis Cabot Lowell introduced his power loom in the 1800s, textile manufacturing contributed a great deal to the economy of Massachusetts. Factories in the state also turned out shoes, leather goods, paper, lumber for building, printed goods, ships, tools, and games. Most of the original factories have shut down. However, new ones have taken their places. Around 10 percent of Bay Staters work in factories manufacturing electrical and industrial equipment, technical instruments, plastic products, paper and paper products, machinery, tools, and metal and rubber goods.

Scientists at the Massachusetts Institute of Technology worked with the US Navy in the 1940s on a project that led to the design of a high-speed digital computer. In 1971, the world's first email was sent from a computer in Cambridge. And, in 2004, one of the most influential social media platforms—Facebook— was developed in a Cambridge dorm room. Now, Route 128, the highway that circles Boston, Lexington, and Cambridge, links technology companies and major universities.

Raymond Samuel Tomlinson created the world's first email application.

A New Textile Hub

The city of Lowell became famous in the nineteenth century for its textile mills, where it churned out fabric that was used to make clothing across the United States. After World War II, however, Lowell's textile factories began to slow down. The city entered into an economic slump, which lasted for much of the twentieth century.

The University of Massachusetts at Lowell now hopes to reinvigorate the city's reputation as a textile hub for the twenty-first century. In the summer of 2017, Massachusetts governor Charlie Baker announced that the university would be awarded over $11 million to establish a Fabric Discovery Center. The Fabric Discovery Center will focus on producing innovative new textiles, which bear little resemblance to the textiles produced in Lowell during the Industrial Revolution. Instead, these new fabrics will be "smart textiles," which will form the basis of new wearable devices. These new fabrics can be used in military uniforms to detect if soldiers are dehydrated or sick, or they can be used in athletic wear to determine the wearer's heart rate.

According to State Senator Eileen Donoghue, "There was a feeling for a long time that textiles were a part of Lowell's past, but not its future. Lowell has become the leader of the technological revolution that once seemed so disruptive." As Governor Baker added, "This investment will ensure we continue to see that success and growth outside of Greater Boston, and that Lowell will have an opportunity to return to the center of the textile industry."

The Fabric Discovery Center planned for Lowell will also work closely with researchers at Massachusetts Institute of Technology in order to bring the latest technologies to textile research and production.

Together they develop products and ideas that benefit the entire world.

Fenway Park

Teams to Cheer For

Massachusetts is home to some of the best-known teams in sports—and some of the most fanatical fans. The Boston Red Sox have been playing baseball in historic Fenway Park since 1912. After an eighty-six-year drought (some people said the team was cursed), the Sox won the World Series in 2004. They won it again in 2007 and 2013. The Boston Celtics, the city's professional basketball team, has won seventeen NBA titles over its storied history. That is more than any other team in the league. The New England Patriots call Foxborough's Gillette Stadium home. In 2005,

As of 2018, the New England Patriots have won the Super Bowl five times.

The Freedom Trail draws millions of visitors every year.

the Pats became the second team in the history of the NFL to win three Super Bowls in four years. They also won the Super Bowl in 2015 and 2017. Massachusetts is also known for its professional hockey team, the Boston Bruins.

Come Visit!

It is not surprising that a state as rich in history and natural attractions as Massachusetts has a thriving tourism industry. Every year, millions of people visit the Bay State to walk the Freedom Trail, a 2.5-mile (4 km) walking path that includes sixteen historic sites. Stops along the trail include the site of the Boston Massacre, Paul Revere's house, and Faneuil Hall. Boston is sometimes called the Cradle of Liberty because of its association with revolutionary colonists such as Samuel Adams.

Visitors to Massachusetts also enjoy fine dining, world-class museums, and cultural events. They experience the best Mother Nature has to offer in every season. The Berkshire Hills are bursting with color during fall foliage time. The region is also home to many internationally famous arts festivals, including the Tanglewood Music Festival and the Jacob's Pillow Dance Festival. In the winter, there is skiing, snowboarding, and other cold-weather activities. In summertime, people from all over the country flock to Cape Cod and beautiful

Nantucket Island

Nantucket Island, where they might visit the quaint towns, go on a whale-watching trip, or relax on the beach.

Each year, around twenty-three million people from other states and countries visit Massachusetts. These tourists help provide jobs for the many Bay Staters who work in hotels, restaurants, stores, and tourist sites. In total, tourism generates about 130,000 jobs in the state. In 2016, these tourists spent about $20.7 billion dollars on food, lodging, and transportation. Massachusetts is obviously an exciting place to visit and to live.

FAST FACT

The first American lighthouse was built in Boston Harbor in 1716 but was destroyed during the American Revolution. A later lighthouse was built on the site in 1783. It is the second-oldest working lighthouse in the United States. Known as Boston Light, it was designated a National Historic Landmark in 1964.

Facebook: Made in Massachusetts

Few inventions have changed how people live and interact with one another as much as Facebook. Facebook was invented by a group of college students, including CEO Mark Zuckerberg, from their dorms at Harvard University in Cambridge. The site was originally designed to support and connect students at Harvard. Since its launch in 2004, however, Facebook has grown rapidly. As of 2017, it has two billion users per month, twenty thousand employees, and an estimated stock value of more than $500 billion. It is one of the largest corporations in the world.

However, Facebook is not just one of the largest social media companies in the world. The company also works on several other projects, including developing virtual reality programs, expanding internet access across the world, and protecting online data. Facebook has also bought

Mark Zuckerberg is pictured here during his college days at Harvard.

Kendall Square will be the site of a new Facebook office.

other popular social media companies, including Instagram and WhatsApp.

Mark Zuckerberg dropped out of Harvard in 2005 to work on Facebook full time. He had already moved his fledgling business to California, where its headquarters remain today in Menlo Park. But now the company is expanding its role in Massachusetts. As of 2018, Facebook plans to open a new major office in Cambridge, Massachusetts, the city where it began. This Facebook office will employ more than five hundred people and will be located in Kendall Square. The neighborhood has been called "the most innovative square mile on the planet" due the number of technology start-ups that are based there. The new office will also house the Connectivity Lab at Facebook. There, teams are working on new aerospace and communication technologies to improve internet access across the globe.

The Massachusetts
State House was
completed in 1798.

5 Government

The Massachusetts state constitution is called the Constitution of the Commonwealth of Massachusetts. The document lays the groundwork for how the state's government works. Massachusetts's constitution is even older than the US Constitution. Adopted in 1780, it is the oldest state constitution still in use today. Like the US Constitution, many amendments have been added to Massachusetts's constitution. These additions have expanded rights for state residents. However, the basic document—and the way the state government operates—has not changed in more than two hundred years.

The elegant State House in Boston is the center of Massachusetts government. However, that is not the only place to find the government of Massachusetts at work. As a former Speaker of the US House of Representatives, Massachusetts congressman Thomas P. "Tip" O'Neill Jr., once said, "All politics is local."

The government of Massachusetts starts with every citizen. Anyone, of any age, can propose a law, and any US citizen eighteen years or older who lives in Massachusetts can register to vote in local, state, and federal elections.

FAST FACT

Four US presidents were born in the state of the Massachusetts. Yet many other presidents have lived in the state. These include Calvin Coolidge, Franklin D. Roosevelt, George W. Bush, and Barack Obama.

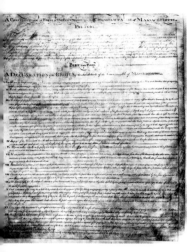

Massachusetts's state constitution dates to 1780.

Levels of Government

There are three levels of government in Massachusetts: city or town, county, and state. Not every county in Massachusetts has its own government—most counties are run by the state government instead. As in other New England states, county government has no authority to tax citizens. City dwellers elect mayors and city councilmembers to govern. Towns elect selectmen. Citizens and their elected officials regularly come together to discuss issues at town meetings, a tradition dating to colonial times. People can also write to their elected leaders to share concerns and opinions. At the highest level of state government, voters elect state senators and representatives, a governor, and other executive officeholders.

As of 2018, there were nine Massachusetts representatives in the US House of Representatives. Like all states, Massachusetts has two US Senators in Washington, DC. Edward "Ted" Kennedy was the fourth longest serving US senator. He was first elected to represent Massachusetts in 1962 at the age of thirty. His career in the Senate spanned four decades, until his death in 2009. In that time, he became one of the US Senate's most influential members.

The United States has two major parties: the Democratic Party and the Republican Party. Ted Kennedy, who was known as "the lion of the Senate," was respected for his ability to "reach across the aisle." He worked well with Republicans as well as members of his own party.

After Kennedy's death, a special election in 2010 determined who would finish out his term in the US Senate. Republican Scott Brown ran against Democrat Martha Coakley and won.

Citizens participate in a town hall meeting in Lynn in 2017.

Massachusetts had a Republican US senator for the first time in more than three decades. Brown served for the remainder of the term. Since 2013, Democrats Elizabeth Warren and Ed Markey have served as Massachusetts's senators.

Ted Kennedy was a Massachusetts senator for more than forty years.

The Executive Branch

At the state level, the governor, lieutenant governor, and other executive officers are elected to four-year terms. The governor, who is the head of state and commander in chief of the state's militia (army), prepares the state budget, suggests new laws, and appoints judges and other department heads. The governor also has the power to sign bills into law or veto (refuse to sign) them.

The Legislative Branch

The state house of representatives and state senate make up Massachusetts's legislature, which is called the Massachusetts General Court. The senate has 40 members. The house of representatives has 160. Senators and representatives are elected to two-year terms. Legislators propose and pass the laws that are ultimately sent to the governor for signature. The governor is the head of state.

Scott Brown filled Ted Kennedy's Senate seat after Kennedy's death.

The Judicial Branch

The state has a system of courts made up of the Supreme Judicial Court, a court of appeals, and many trial courts. The Supreme Judicial Court is the highest court in the commonwealth. Most cases start in a trial court. If there is a disagreement with a trial court ruling, the case

The Supreme Judicial Court is housed in the John Adams Courthouse in Boston.

Second-grade students started a petition to name the ladybug the Massachusetts state insect. Their petition became a law!

may be heard by a court of appeals. Cases may be further appealed to the supreme judicial court. This court tends to hear only cases that raise important legal questions, including whether a law follows or violates the state constitution.

How Are Laws Passed?

The commonwealth has more state symbols than most states. It has a state muffin (corn), a state historical rock (Plymouth), and even a state bean (navy, as the original Boston baked bean). The story of how one symbol, the state insect, was chosen shows how laws are passed in Massachusetts.

One day in 1974 at Kennedy Elementary School in Franklin, Massachusetts, second-grade teacher Palma Johnson told her class about official state symbols. Her students asked why there was a state tree, bird, and fish but no state insect. They decided the ladybug would make an excellent state symbol and that they should try to make it official. The students learned that anyone living in Massachusetts could ask to have a law passed. First, they needed a special form called a petition, as well as a legislator to sign it. So the children wrote to their representative, who agreed to sign their petition.

After that, there was much work to do. First, the petition had to become a bill. It was given an identification number—House Bill 5155—and sent to a committee. The committee discussed whether the legislators should vote on it. Johnson's students went to the State House in Boston to explain why the ladybug should be the official state insect. They told the legislators, "They're so beautiful with their shiny orange backs and bold black spots, and they can be found in everyone's backyard."

Today, it is easier to get involved in how the government is run than ever before, thanks to social media. Both Massachusetts senators, Elizabeth Warren and Ed Markey, have their own website and social media accounts where you can get news about their positions on important legislation. Ask an adult to show you the Twitter accounts of Senator Warren (@SenWarren) or Ed Markey (@SenMarkey). Both senators are very active on Twitter. They regularly update citizens about new legislation through their accounts.

You can also ask an adult to show you the Twitter account of representatives from Massachusetts. These include Representatives Joe Kennedy III (@RepJoeKennedy) and Katherine Clark (@RepKClark). You can send representatives emails through their websites at https://www.house.gov and even request meetings to talk about important issues affecting you.

If you want to get involved in the Massachusetts state legislature, you can do this too. The Massachusetts senate meets at the Massachusetts State House in Boston. As of 2018, it is made up of thirty-one Democrats and seven Republicans. The president of the senate is Harriette Chandler. The Massachusetts senate has its own Twitter account (@MA_Senate), where you can learn about upcoming legislation. You can also learn more about the senate at its website: https://malegislature.gov/Legislators/Senate. The website features a list of all state senators with their contact information.

The best way to become involved in the legislative process is by knowing who your representatives are in the local, state, and federal government. Then, familiarize yourself with these representatives' positions and upcoming legislation. If you feel passionately about a certain issue or bill, reach out to your representatives with an adult's help. If you do this, your representatives will listen to your concerns.

Get Involved!

Senator Elizabeth Warren has an active Twitter account.

The @MA_Senate Twitter account

The committee agreed with the students and presented the bill to the entire house of representatives. The representatives needed to talk about the bill three times before they could vote on it. The class visited or wrote letters to members of the house, asking them to vote for the bill. After the three discussions, the representatives voted to make the ladybug the official state insect.

In order to become a law, the bill had to go to the senate. The children returned to the Massachusetts State House, this time to the senate chamber. They asked for and received the senators' votes. The bill was very nearly a law. It was then printed on special paper called parchment and delivered to the governor.

If the governor signed it, the bill would be a law. If the governor vetoed it, the bill would not be a law. The governor did sign the bill, and the ladybug became the official state insect of Massachusetts.

Land of the Free

Today, it is almost four hundred years since the *Mayflower* landed in Massachusetts. The state continues to be a state known for its laws that protect the freedoms of its residents. In the 1800s, Massachusetts was a center of both the abolitionist movement and the women's suffrage movement. In 2004, Massachusetts became the first US state to legally recognize same-sex marriage. The state also passed universal health care for all of its residents in 2006. Throughout its history, Massachusetts has been at the forefront of many such reforms. Massachusetts continues on this path today.

Glossary

ammunition	The objects (such as bullets and shells) that are shot from weapons.
casualties	Those injured or killed in a war.
charter	A written grant by the ruler of a country or its legislature that creates a company, city, or organization.
commemorate	To celebrate or recognize an event.
committee	A group of people who are chosen to do a particular job or to make decisions about something.
commodity	A raw material or valuable product that can be bought and sold.
democracy	A form of government in which people choose leaders by voting.
environmentalists	People concerned about the quality of the environment, especially pollution.
famine	A situation in which many people do not have enough food to eat.
land grant	A legal document promising to give a certain piece of land to an organization or group of people.
plantations	Large areas of land, especially in hot parts of the world, where crops (such as cotton) are grown.
Second Continental Congress	A meeting of representatives from all of the colonies.
segregated	Relating to the separation of whites and African Americans.
suffrage	The right to vote.
summit	The highest point of a mountain or hill.
surveyed	Measured and examined.
wharves	Flat structures that are built along a shore so that ships can load and unload.

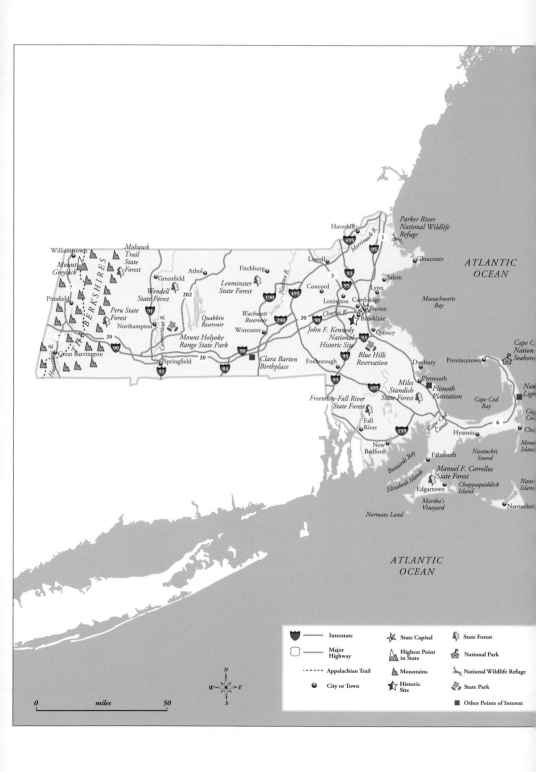

Massachusetts State Map and Map Skills

Map Skills

1. What interstate runs north–south through the western part of the state?

2. What is the northernmost city or town on the map?

3. What is the state's highest point?

4. What point of interest is south of Worcester?

5. To get from Hyannis to Provincetown, which highway would you take?

6. On which island is the Manuel F. Correllus State Forest located?

7. What direction is Lynn from the state capital?

8. Which river is closest to the Wendell State Forest?

9. What two reservoirs are near the center of the state?

10. What bay is east of Plymouth?

Answers

1. I-91
2. Haverhill
3. Mount Greylock
4. Clara Barton's birthplace
5. Highway 6
6. Martha's Vineyard
7. North
8. Connecticut River
9. Quabbin Reservoir and Wachusett Reservoir
10. Cape Cod Bay

More Information

Books

Crane, Cody. *My United States: Massachusetts*. New York: Children's Press, 2018.

Heinrichs, Ann. *USA Travel Guides: Massachusetts*. North Mankato, MN: The Child's World, 2017.

Smith-Llera, Danielle. *Exploring the Massachusetts Colony*. North Mankato, MN: Capstone Press, 2017.

Websites

Commonwealth Museum
http://www.sec.state.ma.us/mus/index.html
View photos, read about exhibitions, take a virtual tour, and more on the Commonwealth Museum's website.

Massachusetts Bureau of Tourism
http://www.massvacation.com
Explore the exciting events and historic sites that the state of Massachusetts has to offer.

The Massachusetts Government
https://www.mass.gov
Learn about working and living in the Bay State from the official Massachusetts government website. You can also find information about elected state officials.

Plimoth Plantation
https://www.plimoth.org
Since 1947, Plimoth Plantation has been operating as a museum to teach visitors about the Wampanoag people and the colonial English settlers in the 1600s. Learn more about their stories at the Plimoth Plantation website.

Index

Page numbers in **boldface** are illustrations. Entries in **boldface** are glossary terms.